BLACK FEZ MANIFESTO
&c.

HAKIM BEY

Black Fez Manifesto

&c.

Hakim Bey

"Let me associate with the
low-brow'd NIGHT"
—James Thomson,
"Winter" (1726)

Autonomedia & Garden of Delight
Brooklyn & Dublin

Salaams & tips-o-the-fez to:
Marcus Boon,
Tanya Solomon,
Ben Meyers,
James Koehnline (for 20 years of collaboration),
Jim Fleming,
Vincent Katz (Vanitas),
authors Stan Gooch and Björn Kurtén, paleolithographers,
the Libertartian Book Club and Anarchist Forum, NYC,
the Colony Cafe, Woodstock, & Shiv Mirabito,
and especially Gordon Campbell of the Academy of Everything is Possible
and Garden of Delight Publications of Dublin and Waterford, Ireland

NYSCA
New York State Council on the Arts

This publication made possible, in part, with funds from
the New York State Council on the Arts, a state agency.

ISBN: 978-1-57027-187-8

Garden of Delight
Dublin, Ireland

Autonomedia
POB 568 Williamsburgh Station
Brooklyn, NY 11211-0568 USA

www.autonomedia.org
info@autonomedia.org

CONTENTS

CROM:
Select Communiqués of the Cro-Magnon Liberation Front

BLACK FEZ MANIFESTO &c.

HAKIM BEY

BLACK FEZ MANIFESTO

We pledge allegiance
to the Ottoman Caliphate
& its long withdrawal into the
                              Mundus Imaginalis
not quite dead but mouldering
                                        Because
our old anarchy fit so well once
                              like Punch & Judy
with such a corrupt & beautiful sultanate
two shadow puppets with bombs on vines
like black melons with sparkling stem fuses
                                        in a garden
of tulips & blood.

                              I could've been
a Bektashi Freemason so there'd be
aesthetic juice on both sides
                              blameworthy cabals
& great hats
                    fezzes
                              dervish crowns
                                        turbans
tombstones in the shapes of hats.
                                        But now
all perfumy caliphal oppression's been replaced
by the unbearably lite
      vapid plastiform airport-international
            techno-gombeen Mormons-in-Space-style
                    cybermillennarian pseudo-Sado-authoritarian
spleen & acedia of the state as tourist trap.

Gog & Magog In Struggle Together
Anarcho-Ottoman United Front
taking the
                    BLACK FEZ
                                    as emblem of our joint
intransigent disgust with the lukewarm
necromantic vacuum of dephlogisticated
                                    corpse breath
that passes nowadays for Empire
                                    & organic death.

A pact or truce between
                    Iblis & Jibra'il
natural & unnatural till once again
we find ourselves perhaps on the
                                    psychic level anyway
                                                    back
in Dr CaligariLand
crumbling palaces bulb-domed with mud
tumbling wooden musky streets where
sated with hookahs and loukoum
we'll resume our
                    war to the knife our
elegant old totentanz.

TOMBEAU FOR ARCIMBOLDO

Gnarled asymmetric cloudlike warped
worn away by weather in blotches, sworls
twisty roots, split rotten fruit
marbled, venous, mottled, buzzing with venereal sweetness
shifting mutable ephemeral, possibly apocryphal
or 'pataphysical, one of a kind, unique freak
alive, sprouting –
                    WHO AM I?
                                    what vegetal power
do these kennings mime? what Vertumnus?
a machine that splices genes (say frog & tomato)?
doppelgänger? antitype? nemesis?
Prime Matter's found on any dunghill but Science
reversing the dreams of Alchemy
turns gold back into turds.
Hint:
In my fomer life as a visual pun
(melon forehead, spring onion hair
peeled cucumber tongue, anthers, stamens, pistils
which become bees that become parts of me,
eyebrow or blush of pubic dust
not molded of clay but pollen)
I
invented a genre unknown to Antiquity.
There are no Ideas only Persons.
It's the exact opposite of allegory:
portentous words, lightning buddha wit, meaning of life, etc.
euphonious gobbledegook, meerschaum, shlag, a
stucco of meringue & persiflage.
"Disturbingly a tiny ant perches on the curled bud
that constitutes her left nipple": —
each word a separate species linked by hypergrammar

conjurations not conjugations
ascensions not declensions:
the numberless Trump blithely poised
to plummet into yet another Defenestration of Prague
perhaps to land in the shit-heap again
perhaps to fly.

[NOTE on "Arcimboldo's Tombeau": Fruit is utopian. Earliest hominids lived
on windfalls & roadkill, the Saturnian Diet. Many utopian fruits come from
one small part of Central Asia: apple & peach (peche, Persian fruit), possibly pears as well; grapes first used for wine, NW Iran 7000 BCE. In China
peachblossoms symbolize Taoist neverneverland. Its fruit confers immortality on Monkey. Peachwood used for magic wands. Apples studied by N.I.
Vavilov (martyred by Lysenko and Stalin) heraldic fruit of Eden, the
utopian prototype. Fourier's vision of apples & pears – the latter esp. a symbol of his Harmonial system of Passional Attraction proportionate to Des-
tinies, with elaborate processions & orgies in the orchards. Bosch characters
live inside fruit in Paradise. Taoist diet all fruits nuts & mushrooms, no grain
or meat. Raw foodists always seem to be getting into trouble over hypersex-
uality & polymorphous perversion as if fruit inspires an eros appropriate
only to a future in which monotheism no longer crushes sexuality & Capital-
ism renounces its monopoly of desire, i.e., when hell freezes over.]

ARCHITOXICOLOGY

If we're going to be poor by Allah let's
be picturesquely poor. Salvage a candyapple
1957 Cadillac & have it drawn by black horses
down the boulevard of our most thaumaturgic aspirations
with hearts open to the infinite throbbing
potential of an idleness money can't buy
the thrill of zilch, the zen of ZeroWork.
Or a steam-powered Airstream trailer
mounted on abandoned weedgrown railroad tracks
or a floating garden built on bales
of styrofoam combed from marine garbage.
Cacagenic & feebly inhibited we already inhabit
the domed forehead of our progenitor
like so many thousands of barn swallows
waiting to be broadcast in a soft
explosion – pinwheels blown at random
at the blustering sky.

ANOTHER PIECE IN THE SHAPE OF A PEAR

Try living on welfare
while waiting for the
Rosicrucians to contact you
by *p'tit bleu* (as in Proust) – a
pneumatique from Sar Péladan
of the Salon Rose✠Croix with
musique by Satie, and see where it
gets you. Ultimately one must fare
forth & cruise the playground, as it
were, if one hopes to be blackmailed with
any kind of rigorous exactitude. We like sea
shells because we can imagine ourselves inside
them, our gelatinous opalescent limbs safe as djinn
in bottles. But what was the face of the clam before it was born if the clam has no face? "Les
Gnosiennes" scuttles across the ocean's flat
floor like a crab on ephedra. In our dove-
gray frock coats & top hats we could
sit here forever waiting for that
pear to blossom.

HYLOZOISM

is a non-negotiable issue.
The quintillion mites aphids e-coli
flagellae & semi-sentient cells that
constitute the colonial siphonophore
writing this text have popularly
& democratically expressed in unanimous
ecstatic waves of applause the unshakable
conviction that the author is a poetic crablouse
in the vast coiffure of the Goddess Ge,
a sybaritic symbiont at the non-stop
symposium of the third mind,
a hermetic parasite, possibly a
brain cell or nerve, a paid witness,
a fanatic sycophantic crony. The Central Committee
in plenary session has embraced the
personality cult of the World as Animal
& will soon be announcing confessions &
show trials for Cartesian behaviorists
cacageneticists & fundamentalist materialists who'll
be sent to mental institutions in Cyberia.

SEMIAUTOMATIC TEXT

I may send my astral double
to live in Ireland. There
he'll fulfil lifetime ambition as
ornamental hermit. Inside my hut
rain will be falling like Dali's Taxi
orchids adorning the mossy
ferny holy well that bubbles
from the hearth. Everything there
is upside down in relation to here
like the antipodes of an hour glass
on a floor of mirrors. There
it's considered eccentric not to be mad
which could become dreary. But
dreariness is essential as is the
entoptic patterning of wet trefoils
that soothes & assails my hypnagogic
pineal in emeraldacious & vedantine
dewdrops of similitude
Anglo-Irish & algae-stained
as a nude statue in Lord
So-&-So's burnt out formal
Georgian walled dead demesne.

NON-JURING SONNET

I chased the ghost of Caspar Schwenkfeld
last of the insubstantialists & champion
disestablishmentarian to a ghost town
in Pennsylvania which in itself
hardly exists yet. This wasn't the first time
pure esotericism encapsulated its own
ineffability in the anguish of such
heretical pullulations or the dark fire
of a problematic materialization on the
plane of the sadness of language.
Tractates by Boehme & Paracelsus
foxed with the blotches of a vast
indifference like liver spots
languished unperused in the vestibule.

and come to think of it the Dead
must've also invented debt
which amortizes or strives ad mortem
long past due date — & usury too,
the sexuality of the Dead. Banks
& tombs alike are vaults passed
down in mortmain undying
as any (dis)corporation – because
the Dead were the first (un)realtors
of privatized space as well – yes
& first to invest in futures
— even money itself — which haunts us now
with papery whispers forever in
long drawn corpse breaths.

Lu Ch'ih Ting Translation

(for J.P. Seaton)

Back
& forth back &
forth wild geese like
ignorant armies stoned on flight:
all this
    waiting around for the Mandate of Heaven
to be withdrawn has become a giant
yawn-fest.
    Fat carp
under the ice restore our
equanimity and imperturbability
when we think of them.
              The
old Chinese curse may you live
in interesting times no longer
applies: who'd've thought
götterdämmerung could be so goddam
dull?
    The geese appear
too addled to fly south
& we await no sudden
summons to high
office.

THE SEVEN TEMPLES OF THE
PLANETARY DEITIES

According to Marsilio Ficino & Cornelius Agrippa
the *Asculapius* of the *Corpus Hermeticum* &
the Puja Shastra of Western Rite Hinduism

On Sundays we are Christians & do no work, or else
only the creative work of Apollo

on sabbath Saturdays we are Jews & do no work for respect
of Jehovah &/or Saturn

Moslems on Friday, the day of Venus, a day
to relax and dally

Jovians on Thor's Day. Some work might be permitted
except for Sufis, as this is our esoteric day off

Wotan's Day, Lugh the Long-armed, Nebo, Thoth, Budha,
Mercury, Hermes Trismegistus: the secret Sabbath of magic

leaving only Mondays & Tuesdays for work. But
Monday is the Moon's – Soma, lunacy, poetry. In Engel's
England workers who failed to turn up for work on Monday
morning said they were observing Saint Monday's Day.

So – Tuesday alone is for labor, Mars rules
fierce & vain exertion.

Like a puff
adder frog or blowfish
this balloon startles you out of yr
quotidian snooze. Cheeks like Shaykh
Roland Kirk's amaze the
groundlings. There's no arguing
with bagpipes. Don't pop a
blood vessel, daddio. Soap
& glycerine & the surface shimmering
like a blowfly's wings – huff
that afflatus for all it's
worth till soaring aloft you
untether from earth & drift
into sheer supposition.

Dr Ralston preached the healthful way
to walk in gentle curves & move
the whole body on circular rotatory vortical
principles of natural whorls & spirals
& go about always on the balls of yr feet
springingly as a child on the way to a promised treat
in upward parabolas like sprouting bulbs
of the most audacious tulips in Turkey
or fireflies in June, the upthrust of
suddenly coherent disorder, a fern
unscrolling itself a mossy tentacle
from fernseed – that metaphor
for the mere imaginary – gentle spore
snailshaped squall or grandiose nebulosity.

[NOTE: See "Hidden History of Ralston Heights, the Story
of New Jersey's failed 'Garden of Eden'," by J. Six, *Archaeology*,
May/June 2004. Tip-o-the-fez to Alex T.]

DIRT SONNET

Bent meaning not straight criminal queer
but kindly bent to ease us
                          the clinamen
the slight obliquity that appears
out of nowhere simply because the Big Bang
is beautiful & loves beauty like the
beast He sometimes simulates & therefore
leans toward the disorder & ordure
we so admire as the very mirror
of His beastliness like some pubescent
Narcissus. What's night soil they asked me
& what possible use could it be
not knowing how the ingenious Chinese
made a thousand flowers bloom in the
moral mortal organicity of the Impure.

Tobacco the most commonly used of all
shamanic plants. Green tea with
sinister connotations of lizardlike
oriental trance states. Spice cabinet
of our lady of sorrows. Sensations of
dizziness almost metaphysical.
Victorian excess. Because
we have purified our environment
of certain malign vibrations we're
all the more susceptible to the
subtleties of these phantastica.
They must come from rare places
where rotting wharves & nodding palms
reveal the future to disordered minds.

InstaSonnet

Do the Inuit intuit by in-wit
how many souls from torrid zones
pass astrally almost nightly
toward their igloos magnetized
by proximity to the axis mundi
or as some say the Hole at the Pole
& do they mind this oneiric tourismo?
No. Because we leave no litter
on the akashic tundra we are
welcomed mythologically with noble
blubber & layers of felt & lard
a cuisine for the disembodied so
an innocent orgy ensues with each
rendezvous at our vedic home in the arctic.

Dr Silence the Edwardian revenant
drifts towards the crime's solution like
sea-wrack with its long tendrils stretched
to the Moon. Neither in- nor deductive
but eluctive and even seductive this
detective revels in the muddied
entangled mumia that englobes &
lurks in otherwise discreet & contradictory
words beneath words in nets of ominous
happenstance & déjà vu. Allah knows
what oriental poisons he's imbibed
in this resembling Holmes who proves
that rationality itself is such a rare estate
it might as well be called a psychedelic experience.

[NOTE: Tip-o-the-fez to Algernon Blackwood.]

Lu Ch'ih Ting Translation

(for Jake)

Master Tea a great reformer
can't be drunk from inferior vessels

& superior vessels demand ever more
celestial brands: Buddha's eyelids

monkey-picked from ridiculous precipices
on strict neo-confucian principles.

Tea spirals out of control then
& begins to move the furniture around

criticize the wallpaper & submit proposals
for radical emptiness, fresh flowers daily

a room of its own with a broom
slanted sunlight on a single scroll

unpolluted water & finally even
conversation both refined & spontaneous.

Your house is actually a UFO
& someday when the command comes
it will lurch aloft still making
that humming noise & float
& fly faster & higher till it
leaves the atmosphere. Let's hope
you're not at home when it
happens. Better be stranded
& lose yr possessions than
raptured upwards & choked
on all that empty waste.

CAROL FOR SATURNALIA

Here in the calendrical interstices
we are shadowed by mysterious agents
like Men in Black but not quite as
menacing who in fact might be Magi
lurching toward some weird Epiphany
stockings stuffed with coal &
broken eggs, some Circumcision Feast
with lurid trappings. Vertigo
overcomes us in the contemplation
of these unnumbered days like the
blankness between oases – vistas
depopulated by replicas of our potential
selves stretched out into n dimensions &
possibly working for other agencies.

A Lunar Garden of Legal Phantastica

(for Jack and Jenny)

I.

poppy, morning glory, moonflower, wormwood, mimosa,
nightshade, belladonna, mugwort, calamus, mormon tea,
Blue Nile lotus, henbane, tobacco, monkshood, grapes,
yew, ivy, laurel

II.

Plaster gnome with painted-on giant dildo will do for
garden Priapus, sine qua non scarecrow of Greco-
Roman psychotropic horticulture. St Anthony of Egypt
(if you can find him) – Saturnian patron of dopers & hal-
lucinogenomaniacs. Blue Virgin with crescent moon on
clamshell doubles as Isis. Must have Mercury – hood or-
nament from old car or Western Union logo – Hermes as
herbmeister. Moon should be present via Turkish flag
perhaps or papier maché Shiva with Luna tangled in his
dreads.

III.

Not necessarily to eat or drink or smoke anything here
except maybe on poppy-hot afternoons a thermos of iced
homemade absinthe – rather mostly just to hang out as
evensong encroaches on lawn chairs beneath the viney
trellises of our faux-Ottoman kiosk & listen. Soak up
mind bending vibrations, keep watch on odd bird be-
havior nearby in the blue hour between dog and wolf.
This should suffice to send guests floating legally home
under pale moons quite re-disoriented.

I was pouring over a manuscript of Tocharian B
the sweat of my pores in the dead
oasis of Turfan when suddenly the shilling
in my akashicometer ran out & I
snapped back on silvery umbilical to
the mere here. The effect was comical
& lingering traces of fading jeers
ejaculated by decayed Manichæans
seemed to tintinnabulate my inner ears
with echoes of the Takla Makan
the Great Nothingness as I tripped
over my own threshold of awareness
& became a gray photograph just
when I was about to decipher it.

NEO-GOLLIST SONNET #__

Snow is heavenly balm for paranoia
almost like semiautomatic writing.
Animals come & animate the afternoon
in a cocoon of youth. Beauty
is under assault but cars are being
torched in retaliation. Snow will
cloak the ruins in aesthetically
pleasing configurations. Children
will cheer the appearance of wolves in
village streets. Thoughts
fill the room like a fog of incense
in an Anglo-Catholic whorehouse.
This is Neo-Gollist weather: thirty-
three degrees on the Freemasonic thermometer.

[NOTE: The word Surrealism was coined by Apollinaire, who appointed the now-forgotten poet Ivan Goll to succeed him as "Pope". But the position was usurped by Breton. At one point Goll punched Breton in the nose in public. When I read this in M. Polizzotti's fine biog of Breton I decided to revive Gollist Surrealism. But it only lasted for an afternoon.]

To Shelley: an InstaSonnet

Civilization in ruins is always a good idea.
Industrial decay has the same
beauty as Persepolis – the melancholy
of vast suffering ended & barely
remembered, like dental pain.
Ozymandias Real Estate (a real sign
seen somewhere in downtown Manhattan)
sells what? the hope that centuries hence
future poets will have the satisfaction
of saying I told you so?
                              brooding
pensively in the picturesque purlieus
of ruined gas stations McMansions
Malls & Interpretive Centers on
the vile tyrannies of long ago?

EVERY MAN WOMAN & CHILD
THEIR OWN TIME ZONE

DEEP SALVAGE

Noseology knows the
pungency of the cosmos, its cheeses,
its toxic wastes & unexpected attars,
its mob connections & minor epiphanies,
its sewers-of-Paris air of romance.
Mountain of cast-offs, rich in capitalist secretions,
sacromonte, tunneled & caved
by spelunkers of the unredeemable,
our Isle of Monte Cristo with its pirate dens
of detritus & soteriological salvage: —
you don't need to inhale to know
with Delphic certainty that the future
belongs to garbage – so why not deal
in garbage futures, invest now in
soon-to-be-booming market for decay.
Sell obsolescence short. Entire small nations
will embrace the economy of garbage.
Garbage ideology. Artificial island
utopias built on shoals of trash,
hot garbage districts generating methane,
empowering the barrios.
Garbage Power. The Will
to Garbage.

On good Saint Monday quote
the Lemonade Ocean & Halleleulia
I'm a Bum. Blue in every sense
dark as they say on Broadway
& intimate as snails kissing in some
softcore Disney naturama, Monday's
a special occasion to increase
the dose, doleful or joyful
wax or wane, Alexander or some
gymonosophist in an urn masturbating,
get out of my light, rentier
or tramp, nature's aristocrats.
Moonday is my darling, a skullcup's
anonymous head dipped in
electrolytic silver gilt for the
delectation of chronically unemployed
but honey-loving drones, gray
in its essence, overcast pearl of
soma, blissful namelessness of
another wasted day.

All the higher animals use drugs &
probably have trouble telling the difference
between para- and metanoia
at the best of times: cows on cider apples
cats on nip slip from fantasia
into aphasia at a single signal
passing cloud,
                    passing moment,
                                        passing show –
lose their ability to speak,
tremble for their identities –
but next day they're back rolling in the orchard
swatting illusory flies. Why?
Because if ghosts are real & the dead
then why not? – or so they think.

ADVENTURES UNLTD.

A bargain-basement Baden-Powell
shambles off to Sham-bhala. Outside the tent
the sirocco or simoom sounds
to our native bearers like the
Beast of American Express. Let's
pretend our travelers cheques were stolen
& finance an expedition to the lost
monasteries of Iblis beneath the
opium dens of Mott St. & Doyers
where the Peking Opera House burned down
in 1911. For once you've arrived
not always already too late but
just in time for whatever treasure Will
to Power can burgle from Character as Fate.

SPHINX MANIFESTO

Balhouba or Abu-Hol the Father of Terror
Chephren the Phix, symbol of the symbolic itself
Alfred Lord Douglas visiting Egypt in 1893 felt
his tremendous paws left no tracks
a female being with a male member
ex parte Leonem & Virginem, Sphinx Mystagoga
enveloped in the veil of enigma
& dissimulation, the spiritual tone
that pervades & holds together the universe
the ether that presses all things like dried flowers
between the pages of Napoleon's Dream Book
Idearum Idea et summa significationis
Sun over the Nile, incestuous offspring
of Echidna & Typhon, rhapsodic dog
crouching on the habitations of the dead –
a language in syllables of granite complaining
that immoral & fatal economics dominates
everything now in 1900 – and as such
the perfect symbol for coins or bills
would be our Capitalist Sphinx – Nature's Key
according to Androgynous Freemasonry, compound
of earth air fire water in a single monster
flooding of the Nile, grotto of Revolution
queen of the pirates concealed in a little box
wiping out with its tail the impressions of its feet.

[NOTE: thanx & tips-o-the-fez to Zadkiel,
W. Goth Regier, Athanasius Kircher, Bakunin, Sar Péladan, et al.]

CREEPY SENSATION

People of the Future are reading us
now & envying our thenness
evil eyes skimming our pages
blighting our crops & wilting
our infants, gnashing their gaze
over our intimacy with species long extinct
their baleful rays of yellowgreen bile
seeping back into our long days
siphoning off layers of poignancy
sucking & sipping it forward into their
flavorless millennia. Bastards of the Future
bulbbrained GM-model clone fuckers
release our hostages, redeem our hocked
sensations or suffer the consequences.

TIRESOME SONNETS

OR,

LASSITUDINARIANISM

I.

My aura's out of whack – I need a
Blavatskian therapeutico-pharmacopoeian
Bishop Leadbeater to beat the lead
from my head with
14 karat carrots to keen-sight me some
golden bi-focals like Joe Smith's –
not so much for clarity as dazzle.
Hung-over from my hang-over I invoke
St. Monday patron of slackers.
Alas for the Order of the Eastern Star
& its teen messiah – gloomy
Monday theosophical fog looms
above sad fond memories of Bombay
keeping me home from school in bed all day.

II.

An epyllion
in the tired tarnished
mauve & silver mode of Nonnos of Panopolis
or Dracontius (poet laureate of the African Vandals)
tinselly epicule set in
Imaginal Egypt or languid Carthage
where they wear jasmine behind their ears
in the bazaars & lean on lampposts
mooning dreamily into space even today
has proven too tiresome.
Christians are coming. Count Belisarius
sets sail from Byzantium.
The last 15 minutes of Late Antiquity
allow but a few fugitive lines…

III.

Dionysus as Savior makes a
dangerous messiah, drunk & bi-sexual
panther skins & highheel'd buskins
thinks Nonnos, & in that sense
not so different from Jesus.
                              He sighs
& gazes out the window. Sun
blazes over the Serapeum as usual.
Dazed, he draws back the shade
of rustling rushes. Nothing has changed
since the First Dynasty except for
universal craquelure, a seepage of heaviness
astral & maleficent that suffuses
everything.
                What shall he work on today –
his *Dionysiaca*…or his *Versification of the*
                              Gospel of John?

Open Letter plea to fanciers &
messenger pigeon services please
contact the undersigned seeking
means to communicate & disseminate
by silver doves by breathing opals
in the bated air certain tractates
on alchemies too delicate for machines
to transmit thru lifeless geometries
& sterile algorithms. Only blood
can carry these letters only
something that arrives in beauty
& biblical secretiveness with
soft explosive flutterings like
an anticipatory heart.

SCHIZOPOESIS

I is an other says Hermit Crab
& not even my own species, this
squatted character armor nacreous
but excreted by someone else
entirely. No communiqué claiming
credit for any outrage will ever
emanate from this Captain Nautilus
this two-horsetail Pasha down in
submarine Bosnia. He huffs
his hubblebubble each puff
a speech-balloon with no semantic content
that rises to the surface, pops
& releases a whiff of sobranie
from the Balkans of the deepest trenches.

Meanwhile
a single word engraved on granite
gravestone like an epitaph but with
no name, just
                    Meanwhile
a novel in which everything
happens simultaneously recited
in 5 minutes by 500 readers reading
at once
              Meanwhile
I'm holding on listening to
vapid synthesizers waiting
waiting for the other shoe to drop
the other bomb, the one that
destroys time but leaves
everything else intact: the big
                    Meanwhile.

Dogs bark – geese honk – yr basic Dutch moment
slips between interstices of an otherwise
homogenized lo-cal vitamin-enriched
American day. Machines die
machines rot & decompose like
road kill. A dirty interregnum
a sluttish kitchen-Irish hiatus intrudes
between two monoliths of unpockmarked
plausibility consisting of the rest of the
day & the rest of the day stretching
hygienically left & right as far as
eye can see thru unshed tears
where no ice is ever harvested &
dogs are edited from the ambient mix.

NEOTENY

1.

Stupefying idleness natural to
childhood must be strenuously defended
throughout a mothhood devoted by
hoi polloi to reproduction of labor.
Every day of unemployed turpitude
is a little revanchist ploy against the
cubal universe or square of all squares:
drawing pirate maps with Johnny & Billy
(real names).

2.

Inherit yr little puddle & be independently
poor but amphibious. Losing yr tail &
growing it back is the act of an atavistic
carny geek but it's America's most
charming party trick & has its
lordly moments. Play for pay.
Worship the Infant of Prague who became an
egg again just as you drift off to sleep
in the green sunlight of yr natal marsh.

3.

Thou Shalt Want Ere I Want

                every afternoon wasted

in the park

                must somehow be funded.

4.
IWW means
I Won't Work –
our enemies are correct.

5.
Once in the ruins of Pang Yang where "tri-racial
isolates" wallowed in savage sloth
fishing & hunting & moonshining applejack
sunk in superstition & ecstatic incest
I had a vision of the lizard god.

6.

Axolotl the Nahuatl "water toy" dark
salamander of Mexico
attains sexual maturity & breeds
while remaining in the larval stage
just like the bohemian revolutionary.
Seven sages of the bamboo grove seven
sleepers seven Rip van Winkles &
his dog, all working
underground for the dictatorship of cruel
green-eyed blond children from Outer Space.

7.
In the Garden of Neoteny
I'm always sniffing the intimate methane scented
frog haunted marsh behind the chicken farm.
Black mud flecked bare feet.

8.
Or frog sticking in the marsh, not this
sclerosis. Bone idleness is itself a
strenuous vocation necessitating a passion
for dressing up & passing out.
In the true sense
of surcease from sorrow
dragonflies hovering over the swamp
L. Frank Baum the inspirational speaking
trumpet of our wunderkindergarten.

9.
Must we have a Programme?
Child zeks of Cyberia
throw off yr theosophical rays & revert
to the mystic stink of the Reptile House
ammoniac hot snake thrills
of recurrent prepubescence.
Seize the day of inadvertency.

PLOT

They're planning an 8-lane by-pass over the Past & you the handsome young Emergency Archaeologist must quickly rescue a few shattered fragments from oblivion. Just as a mastodon can be inferred from a few bones by osteomorphological intuition so you grope to reassemble these shards jigsawed to randomicity by bulldozers & dynamite into some relic of the Palace of Memory. Organ music UP. It's a magical papyrus buried by spirits 40,000 years ago revealing the secret rituals of an Order not quite human. Palengenesis can recreate a living rose from its ashes according to Paracelsus as sweat beads your noble brow. Science is baffled. In strangely hyperrealist scenes you seem to visit torch lit caves where Emblems flicker in mushroom light & chants filter down from other dimensions in a synasthesiac gesamtkunstwerk of erotic-esoteric enigmas. Suddenly you find yourself afloat in an ivory boat on a marble lake of lotuses at the Summer Palace outside Peking in 1903 & beside you the Dowager Empress "Old Buddha" is eating frog congee & listening to the Imperial Water Music Ensemble. She turns & points a five-inch lacquered fingernail at you & intones a Manchu mantra bestowing upon you the power to smite enemies with hideous boils & rashes just with words. To raise storms. Charm snakes. Wake up! she hisses, you're cursed to search forever for Hidden Ireland. The Order of Bards has set sail without you for Tir na Nog the island of youth & evaporated in Jacobite conspiracies in the late 18th century. And indeed things look bleak as you find yourself back at the dig: concrete has been poured like leprosy over the whole site & lawyers have arrived with writs of cease & desist. And the Artifact is missing, presumed stolen by sinister forces. Suddenly you find yourself the High Priest of a religion that exists only in the unseen world of your memory, lost & accused of schizophrenia by your erstwhile colleagues, reputation shot, grandmaster of a powerless cabal, prophet of a future that should have been but won't.

ARMS

Frog as sexual singer
totem brahmin with bullhorn
treble alto tenor bass
queer episcopalian of the swamp
green organist or onanist
of Smoky Mary's Oratorio of the mists & meres, the
were-frog runs out to dance in javanese rains on
ritual cannibal Catholic legs with garlic & butter
or basil & red chillypeppers – a
Neanderthal with goggle eyes
who lurks beneath bridges
on foggy days & pounces out
to suck victims' tongues

and the other one is the crane
or his local congener the blue heron
the antiquarian of the Bestiary
our Scottish Thoth. Along
the famously haunted back creeks of our ecotone
he flies low & slow & alone as blue
evening itself
              closing lid of the
very jewel box of Captain Kidd
the treasury of twilight.

THE AROMAL SLEDGEHAMMER

An amuletic prophylaxis
rain's alembic
cocoons & soothes
the agitated Muse.
The mechanick loom
the Luddites wrecked
was in a sense the first computer
just as the first hand-loom
was the womb of the dialectic.
A soft ball-peen
for a soft machine
like rain on a tin roof
insists that manifestoes can be
a kind of slow terrorism.

SHOE DREAM

Morning rain traps sleep's effluvia
beneath the belljar of its pallium –
a woeful era for the shoe lover
except in Buster Brown's dream dredged
from unassuaged REM states even
as bureaucracy recapitulates
the nightmare of bad design.
Hermetically sealed, it releases its
reluctant subfusc crepuscular funk
in a whiff like the pfft of a pierced coffee can. Then
the shoe dream walks away from Dreamer's p.o.v.
& vanishes down a long perspectival spillway
in a double atmosphere of sad satori.

O makebelieve Ireland
O Atlantean remnant
you will never be wholly free
while the Romano-British Empire still
holds sway you'll always need an IRA
or Fenian Siblinghood of Hibernian
ci-devants & deviants O cradle
of poetic terrorism of cuprous & smarigdine
mist-glisten'd megaliths &
moss-browed Sweenys browsing on
cold watercress & nettle soup
porter & oysters – a Cro-Magnon dish –
we demand our right of return to the bardic bog
& a rain-ticket on our portion of the cosmic pig.

Our Demi-Messiah Fourier informs us
work is not substitute for sex but rather foreplay
a passion suspended beyond completion –
Jam Today. The moment of being possessed
more precious than possession
— the whole history of the pear in each sip
from blossom to rot each season with its
arcane ritual in the orchard
a Sexual Angelicate with its own
self invested hierophants in a veritable phalanx
of 18th century spunk & know-how
stakhanovite avatars of the unquantifiable
but nevertheless mathematical exactitude
of falling in love with and on the job.

Ideally I'd like to be an
intensely local poet the kind
that publishes in the town newspaper's
                "Poetry Corner"
remembered fondly by the County
Historical Society & recited at
Grange picnics. Perhaps a pageant
for the public elementary school or
                an epic
printed privately for the author
still to be found on the shelves
of the village library where the
old lady tells anecdotes about my
                bouts of alcoholism
but represses the other scandals
which were never proved anyway.
Every once in a while a strange phrase will
jump off the page & stick with you like
                a personal memory.

"...the monstrous significance of unthinking jubilation."
■ Max Stirner

Lucky I'm not one of those low-life novelists who preys
on family for ichor or else certain aunts of mine
would long since have been drained.
Where have all the aunts gone taking narrative with them?
They themselves have retreated into fiction
heaven or Florida, background extras
in some neo-noir *roman policier*
about suicide or ecocide in the Everglades in
a Wellesian long-shot of blue-perm'd old ladies
sipping hi-balls at a bank of one-armed bandits
in a hell realm designed by Piranesi.
No one retires to Florida for the sun that engine of entropy
they go for the air-conditioning
& the bitter satisfaction of evading closure.

Every animal is a gesture
hardwired into the garden of allegories
able to sway the minds of millions
like Mandrake the Magician because
if animals are good to think with then
humans with animals' heads have a
head start deeper than speech. But
what a cocktease this storm – so
hesitant – like air-brushed porn. Let
some other sage cultivate this Jove
who can't get it up this swan
that never comes to cover us
with wings of rain.

A lot of dutch bowling up there
in the hills but no cum shot.
Rip is wrapped in dead skin
a cocoon that'll never open.
The hills are a dryness
unable to ripen.
He won't be back to see the Future
& his dog is dead
long since dead.

"No Ontology Without Pharmacology"
— tee shirt by Freddie Baer

Nobody who's done a lot of drugs is going to bother to challenge the Intelligent Design Hypothesis – their only question is going to be – cui bono? Basing the project on Nothing doesn't mean no project. God begins with "an inordinate fondness for beetles" and meanings but soon lets it slide. The Quantum observer ceases to fiddle between particle & wave and simply *assumes the position.*

Earth needs more parking lots
the way you need more patches of asphalt
grafted to your face & genitalia
so that tiny wee flying saucers
from the Planet of Alien Germs
can park on you like the flies
E. Dickinson heard buzzing
round her head when she died.

Behind the loading dock
of the bankrupt superstore somewhere
in the Hell Zone late at nite
& even later in the whole historical
process of decline nothing has
ever died. Something dead
would be downright homey.
One ragged chicory blooms blue
thru the concrete providing the only
potential death to touch this
vacuum with any last breath.

COMMENTARY ON "IMPRISONED WITH THE PHARAOHS"

by HOUDINI ghosted by H. P. Lovecraft
Weird Tales, 1924

(tip-o-fez to Hans Plomp)

A cheesy messiah for the bumbling proles
Houdini finds his gospeller in HPL
his pseudo-Dionysian Joe Smith
Lion Bull Eagle Man Bible as Sphinx
or sphincter. Straight is the gate indeed.
Adorned with cacaglyphs our chamber
of excremeditation sinks like some
vast pneumatic Parisian ascenseur the size
of Shea Stadium. Dyspeptic loneliness
alone allows our Lovecraft to recraft
the gloomier bits of Valentinus into
this disilluminated Hymn of the Pearl.
Après the Cagliostran chills all ropes fall away &
we rise to the surface like an embolism into
                          the mesosphere.

SOMNIUM

1.
"Come to prayer
 Prayer is better than sleep"
             — Dawn Azan (Hanbali version)
"but the sleep of the Knowers is worth more
 than the prayers of the merely pious"
                          — Hadith

Magnetic Sleep
aslant to the Multiverse
in a beam of theta waves
Morpheus the Merciless
sips

2.
chamomile & melatonin
poppies & hot milk
milk with a skinskim
of yellowish cream

beneath a quilt stuffed with Indian grass
in a hammock of Indian Summer
with a pillow blessed by Ibn Sereen
the Father of Islamic Oneiromancy on

an island of lotus eaters
soporific with ebony halls of
silent black marble & moonlight
highlighting the limbs of Hermaphroditus

"assumes the shape of an egg"
& performs the opposite of hatching.

DOG OF THE SUN

the days are our slaves.
We set up maquiladoras on the Moon.
An albino persian cat.
Watch yr fingers the Sun's dog's
cavorting with its little pal
Nicola Tesla.
On the esoteric level — pow —
a K-O blow rare in this
junior flyweight division
wrists like slender white stalks
borne down by the heavy flower of their
pendulous gloves.
Puppy vs. Kitten
the sky as gym
clouds as cigar smoke
stale & blue.
Would you like to see
naked boxeo
Sun & Moon in the
same pale heaven?

A fine day for abduction by eagle or erl-king
whilst the snow lies roundabout
        crisp as a Norwegian
                but shallow
as social democracy:
            resonant hurrahs
                 cut off
from contact with the Demiurge
weighed down by gravitons the size of
           bowling balls: March
kites held tremblingly
            straining their own tissue
in eagerness to be uplifted.

One virulently violent violet moonlit night
Luna honked across the sky
crazy white goose celestial cadillac.
Silently blue houses
ran in her wake, barking dogs that
lost their voices. Now we know
death is boring & the dead couch potatoes
glued to tubes forever on hospital beds
every window leaking Emergency Code Blue
from its poison moon. And
the houses never move.

Winter as Bakunin's Beard
stirs up DER STURM! & sweeps
all definitions into blurred whorls
& hyperborean drifts
drips ice water over
silver spoon thru sugar
sips his Green Fairy
cruises the altocumuli
in his flying kettle
seeding the busted clouds
with eldritch chemicals.
The Horse of Winter
speaks with his mouth:
Revolutionary Soteriology.

A Floral Fantasia

for Janissary Band & Loudspeaker

Unfurl once more the moth-eaten
banner of Eleusis a terrible
beauty born-again so to speak
a Rapture toward Tellus & not the
pearly gates –
          fundamentalist neo-pagans
tree-huggers with guns
grim as Holy Vehm
dance horses of the Sybarite Cavalry
proud as lilies
          Forward!
or, if not, then
          Backward! down to an
Arts-&-Crafts Kropotkinite vision
of Spring as War of the Flowers
or War of the Massed Choirs

mourning & solitude
narcotized narcoleptic necromancy
shamanism as Arctic Hysteria
spite
      spleen
          the virtues of Winter
piled up in the sink
aquamarine with penicillin
its brooding Lenin-in-Zurich cogitations
among the Nietzschean mountains &
Nechaeyevist ozone where
only our Osama ibn Sabbah
gaunt doe-eyed Winter with the scythe
could stew such black roots –
last living devotee of
Flower Power.

Geomancy places tombs
to channel telluric vibrations
over time. Shall we have our winter dead
under the hearth & near enough for
colloquy – or be Hindoo
transubstantialists instead?
They weigh down the corners of the map
with their heavily therapeutic dust.
The map is not the territory
and yet it is.

A Weeping Thaw

> "Ye sons of Indolence, do
> what you will."
> — James Thomson
> "The Castle of Indolence" (1748)

hero of yr own gothick novel!
vivid life of hedgerows apiaries
                    corncribs lightning rods
Chladni Diagrams nitrous oxide
cucumbers glistening with salve!
Yr own Gnostic fragment!
cankers on the spirit of the bland
            smiley face of heroic modernism!
Cut off three days by flood we await
our SSI & remittances, admiring our
wounds in the yellowed mirror,
living out of tins like an ocean liner
in slo-mo thru an ocean of snow,
an ocèan liner that dare not speak its name,
a parasite gone long in the tooth.

FRAGMENTS

Tea was given late to humanity perhaps to compensate for the erosion of a certain intimacy with nature. Effortlessness now demands some effort, attention some tension.

The Old Mole is the master of "is".

Snow: heraldic gesso for the autonomous image.

Snow saves children from the schoolroom like Wm Blake.

The North, sensing our yearning, comes south to meet us.

Winter's harem feminizes us
inside the house discreetly.
Stormbound we turn Turke
gender blurs behind night's chador
the perfect drag. Our husband Boreas
sighs with his culture of shame.
We lose our inhibitions
with our faces & give way
to seraglio vices in our
funky purdah.

Cold Cage Paste
              Purple Sunshine
                            Big Smoke
Slice of Crow
              压丸 *"ya pian"*
                            Black Fragrance

the cloud with its own brain
enclosing the room with sound
of rain a hundred year old egg
translucent as a blackened lamp
with a black yoke, Fabergé
swan in a snowscape & a pair
of parchment yellowed hands handling
the silver gun like crab claws
toying with rotten meat. *When it's stagnant*
mountains & mist emerge from distant sea
Swallowing Clouds & Spewing Fog
It's always the Right Time for such an
                    object of lovesickness.

[Tip-o-fez to Zheng Yangwen]

GIMME

my jeweller's loupe-garou
my louche one-eyed goblet
of the far-seen eye
my vulture my mouse
in green spectacles
my aggies
&
my fly whisk
for the cobwebs of previous
misincarnations
of the green parrot that
bit me
&
I'll analyze thunderbolts & scry
entrails – a fry-up for the gods
& pick Lotto numbers
&
sit fatly in front of my
garish tent be-fezzed & hookah'd
hooked up to pyramid phrenology
waiting for you to cross my
cheiromantic palm with something
sincerely heartfelt & worth about
three hundred dollars.

MONTGOLFIER AT THE COUNTY FAIR

that Sacred Heart that
apple from outer space
beefily wreathed with thorns
teleports itself & spritzes its
cinnamon blood on greasy oleographs all
over tantrik Italy.

Count von Zinzendorf wanted to crawl
into the Side Wound like
a Montgolfier gondola lined in
rosepetals & spareribs

a pink flamingo.
Icarian Infantas tour
the Noösphere
on flammable airs like baby spiders
surfing the zephyrs
like the Lady Sawed In Half.
That Heart laughs, a

dazzling
rubrous carbuncular car descending
earthward, burning but
not consumed. The
passengers emerge both shaken & stirred
like overdetermined martinis: all rosey &
spangled with alien fruit.

MAD SWEENY

Clustered alone round the faded hearth
Sweeny thinks he remembers being
driven woodsqueer eating watercress & nettles
till he became a kind of green man
himself. The college bell tolls emptily
Tristan Tristan driven frantic with
love potion flees to the forest
filthy & naked. Was that me?
Surely the zoning code would
forbid it or rangers would soon come round
with citations for violating
protected wilderness. Surely by now
I'd be in therapy no longer bothered
by Isolde or the horrors of war.

Dr Brink (1754 – 1843)

The Enlightenment is a Good Ship Lollipop of which
we're the rattus norvegicus scuttling
ashore in rain-light sighing sauve qui peut.
Our guru knew that Dr Brink of Kingston
his enchanted forest now reduced to a few
tombstones in a suburban back yard backed
up to the exit ramp for Route 202
will supply us with graveyard grisgris
quack-spagyric brews & slews of roots
& simples. Someone must've been through
before us dropping breadcrumb clues
& influencing us with rural cunning
to pose as cryptic potentates &
nibelungize the Scenic Hudson view.

GHAZAL

Anarcho-monarchist direct action:
sit on throne facing auspicious direction
doing absolutely nothing.

The wind rose itself can make any
two bit oasis the Mecca
of wayfarers.

Magnetic storms confuse our sense
of direction with pollution across the whole
hermetic spectrum.

I lost you. You've forsaken
the ancient secret of crystal radio
for an alien wavelength.

I know you're the Pole of the Age
& salvation depends on finding you
but like a top

wobbling entropically I've fallen
out of hopelessness & no longer recall
which way is up.

Everyone
in the country
has a Neighbor From Hell
suggesting that an average
of one out of every four American
households is possessed by demons
or extra-terrestrials. On the
global level America itself is
the Neighbor From Hell
noisy vulgar malevolent
the stench of our barbecue
drifts across nextdoor nations
wholesale & our shrieking laughs are
heard around the world.

FINANCIAL DISCLOSURES

or
the budget of poesy
or
Eros as starving beggar
or the Danäe of the Rhetoriticians
Break the bank o' my heart
worthless as a paper fan
on a sultry day in hell

1.
Two ways to be vulnerable
vis-à-vis the universe
pay for a classified ad
"please put a spell on me
p.o. box so-&-so" – or
be a bank that fails
Ah the giddy thrill
desperate punters run amok on bourse
& we lift off borne aloft on
waves of panic like a box-kite
on hawk's-breath
pilot of nothing.

2.
O Carlo Ponzi secret pharaoh
builder of the first pyramid scheme
am I the John Law of hopeless tulipomania
irrational euphoria
secular pentecostalism
sickly platonizing &
emotional cheque-kiting?
Kite-fighting: you soar get caught

entangled cut loose fall
captured or lost
but for an afternoon you pierced the cerulean
azure overturned turquoise bowl, you
broken hearted dragonfly – a
vast investment in blue
& nothing to show for it
but these clouds.

3.
Poetry is weather that stays weather
a river that ices over for years at a time

"As good a right as the Queen" of course
but no collateral: bankrupt as valentine

pink as cheek on brisk day.
It's tender but is it legal?

On yr threshold the dust of yr threshold
increases like interest on debt

exponentially faster than inflation itself
till stars & meteors start to whizz past our heads

& we're falling in free fall toward the
flesh tone heart of the pluriverse.

4.
The besotted & cunning lover lends at 10 or 20 times the
amount of actual deposits. Our deepest vaults hold nothing
but dead moths that never knew the ecstasy of burning to
cinders in the lamp of the beloved's glance.
     I'd love to ruin myself
     financially for you like the
     great lovers in Balzac we all
     secretly admire. How often the ardent
     make mental reservations about
     bonds & real estate! Only Majnun

                              the fou d'amour
              can spend money like spunk.
On some level we know we're being conned but we go along with it
because the immediate pay-off quells all hesitation. Lovers live in the
leap itself. Issued in Weimarian zillions our Taoist Hell Bank notes
exist as money only in the smoke of their disappearance in the furnace
of the Imagination. Credit & credulity: a match made in the very
heaven where money goes when it dies: a certain kind of genie that re-
sponds only to a certain kind of Aladdin. The sutra of suing for yr af-
fections in the chancery of verse: yr eternal debtor.

Jubilee never comes. Debt mutates into peonage. Crushing abstrac-
tions are handed down like family heirlooms. Formerly one could seek
sanctuary in certain cathedrals & shrines. But then temples all became
banks of universal credit symbolizing debt as cosmic principle. In this
case the beloved must turn bank robber. Metaphor will force you to
confess yr crime. Security is non-existent. I can feel you zeroing in like
a lovely vulture over the town dump. But to be robbed now would be
the salvation of this psychic S-&-L which otherwise faces Chapter
Eleven.
                    Casuistic allegorizing's better
                    than nothing & nothing's what you get
                    from other dealers, pal. Go into hock
                    to yr own quivering monadic sensorium
                    pay off deep debts of honor
                    lost pascalian wagers
                    short of sheer abscondage.
                    Buying back paper with new paper
                    always ends in crash – but
                    our secret lies in the certainty
                    that irrational exuberance
                    is an end in itself.

          5.
          The pudding of truth
          pink as a shell grotto scented
          with peony talcum, this
          fiat currency will buy
          a sleigh lacquered blue

drawn by a white pony
a baby squirrel
a weekend in Zamboanga. Come,
ruin my dull rentier liquidity
& we'll roar off together into the lengthy
Annals of the Badlands.

"To be blunt, I preferred to
steal than to be stolen from."

— Alexandre Jacob, anarchist burglar
Statement to the Court, Paris, 1903

In the back room of an
                    occult bookstore
near the Pantheon a groupuscule called
ZARATHUSTRA'S REVENGE concocted the
                    bomb plot but
the infernal device turned out to be
                    a dud but regret
is at least an emotion. I was there
& I am still there
a ghost to myself.

Huckleberry Finn

O.D.'d on Ritalin™

& Tom Sawyer

grew up to be a lawyer.

FAILURE AS THE LAST POSSIBLE OUTSIDE

> "I trailed that bad boy
> who whistled hands in pockets till
> between the houses the Red Sea parted
> & two waves arose & I was Pharoah
> & he was the Jews"
>   — Apollinaire
>   "La Chanson du
>   Mal-Aimé"

dedicated to
Albert Pinkam Ryder
(1847–1917)

> "It is little to be wondered at that he
> gives us neither living figures nor even
> a gallery of pleasing portraits or statues,
> but rather a faded & overcrowded tapestry,
> moving a little now & then as the breath
> of his sickly & unwholesome fancy
> stirs it."
>   — H. J. Rose, "Mythological
>   Introduction" to the
>   *Dionysiaca* of Nonnos

I.

Somewhere there's a blasted heath for us
a dust bowl too depressed beneath
midwestern oceanless horizons for
anyone to hear our muffled orisons or
an American Chernobyl where we can
roam free at the risk of a few mutations.
I am the Mayor of Love Canal, its Abbot Nullius
my discourse poison & my weeds
rank & faggy. I am damp dynamite

outdated detonationless furred
with mildew but still with all my original
bad intentions. We must learn
to view Nature as that which is
abandoned unreal estate where the
old elementary school crumbles away &
winters are as stupid as chickens

II.
badland so boring that even
the police fall asleep on its borders
there's where we'll make our Hejira our Hajj
our Exile & Return in one
fell swoop, the desert blooms
with phosphorescent succulents
the prairie's restored by relentless
entropy itself – benign neglect.
I am that Peter the Hermit who always
preaches the Children's Crusade
secret agent of the Saracens in the pay
of Istanbul but haven't heard
a word from HDQ since 1924.

III.
In the rose garden metaphor

the lover plays one of the Blameworthy secret confraternity that masks
its profound piety in public drunkenness & obloquy, one of the Clever
Ones stealthy enough to bib the wine of heresy & not get caught – a
tantrickster's tightrope act above a chasm of bourgeois mediocrity &
sleeping policemen

In science fiction terms, picture

a future where whole minor former 3rd-world nations & midwestern
states are enclosed as literal garbage dumps by sinister forces of the
Global Imperium, no-go-zones secretly illegally still inhabited by New
Mud People, savage bricoleurs evolving strange ghostdance cults &
language mutations

In theoryspeak

the endlessness of the End of History eventually degenerates (in both
the spicy & the eugenic sense) in a Zenonian precession toward the
possibility of Will to Power as Disappearance – a new trialectic arising
out of the mulch of sheer insignificance, neither overtly criminal nor
covertly conformist, resistance as evasion, vagueness, evaporation, ten-
uosity, reticence, escapism, horizontalism, paradoxical productivity of
all that refuses to be computed, that which "doesn't count" – a weird
penumbra that somehow slips past panoptic surveillance by its obvious
fatuity & futilitarianism: failure as the last possible Outside

the Silentium Hermeticum

symbolized by the child Harpocrates finger to lips in a gesture of *sshh* –
or of bewildered innocence – the divine fingersucker – the golden em-
bryo's infantine goblinesque & perfect redness – imagination as chaotic
attractor – an alchemy within language itself that seeks transmutation
but never finds it except in the seeking – words of Adamic & oneiro-
critical significance that evaporate into gibberish whenever we awake
from the trance of self into the sleep of otherness: failure.

> IV.
> The editorial we therefore propose a certain
> dandyism of failure
> connoisseurship of the unspectacular
> the poor & sad
> clumsy clandestinity that recognizes itself
> by childish pseudomasonic high signs.
> Figuratively speaking we
> retreat to our Airstreams in the Pine Barrens
> guerillas who never risk defeat
> by never engaging. In simile
> you see us lolling on broken couches
> on overgrown lawns vacantly
> contemplating the empty marsh
> & take us for trailer trash when in truth
> we're the Shaolin monks of the new millennium
> disguised as outcaste beggars & percolating
> thru the cracks in the Empire.

FINANCIAL SONNET

Invest yr Bank of Hades billions
in the Imaginal Wall St. of money gone
to heaven. Sipping the
green wines of science fiction with
futures so neoplatonic you can smell them suddenly
I'm the George Soros of the
Invisible World of numismatic
rhapsodomancy. Bankside lots on Lethe
abandoned factories on Phlegethon 're
so far out they're in again
like say Christian Socialism or
Wildwood NJ with its elephant shaped towers.
We lost our ghostshirts on the stock
exchange of revery. Don't Say No To
                    The Muse of Investment.

BIBLIOMANCY

> "Oppose
> Book
> Worship"
> — Mao Tse Tung

This book changed my life but
unfortunately no one else ever
read it maybe a few lonesome
cowboys with their emersonian guitars
once annotated dog-ear'd underlined
spatter'd margins with exclamations & stars
in a kind of omniomancy or
sortilege by absolutely everything, or
both at once, social-realist self
portrait with pipe dog & elbow patch
for colportage into regions
beyond the Pole always hoping
to reach that one
perfect reader.

AN OLD
MOOR'S ALMANACK
FOR MANIACS

for Monsters
well-loved by children who
dream of being rapt away and
for Aspiring Changelings
& superstitious Old Crones
who believe cats re-incarnations
of ancient Romans
with
A Rough Calendar
guaranteed to cause Inefficiencies
& Unexplained Delays
plus
useful lies, excuses, procrastinations
101 Ways to weasel out of Work
A Very Poor Book of Hours

We're against Daylight Savings
& even Time Zones. Clocks (if any)
should be set to geolocal standards
in a sinuous chronomap of
chronoweather & synchronicities —
a serendipitous jigsaw veering
toward slippage. You for example
are one of the Days of Spring
a blossom of the Appleseed Militia.
I picture you in your green shirt
practising knots & marksmanship
reading up on homemade bombs.
A special feature & several homilies
on farming lifted from Virgil in this issue
are meant for you to decipher with your
Special Agent Kit & well-thumbed copy of Theocritus.

NOTE ON A PHRASE OF MARX

The opposite of melting into thin air would be
solidifying into fat air like stigmata in a soulfood kitchen
angel of annunciation in the buttery dutch light of
an embarrassment of riches, specter at the greasy banquet
handwriting on the wall in an oleaginous haze of benzoin & aloes.
Somewhere in between these two states
in that rarest of forms – slime –
unknown on Pluto or Mars we find
the manifesto as conjuration or contagion
words that rub off & scent your clothes
inks made of bile compounded with civet
stinks you can nearly see, ancient lard dampnesses that persist
till mildew spreads & dies & spreads & dies –
oil of old house, a presence palpable.

BARON MUNCHAUSEN

The New Male Muse
our poetic *uſtad*. Didn't
they used to call printshops
devils' chapels? How can you
"Reach Out & Touch Someone" with a telephone
except as a murder weapon?
The hot-air balloon was stolen
from Hermeticism like everything else
so ho-hum. The Baron's childhood
resembles our own in its gawky oneiro-
onanistic reticence & hesitancies
since Dr Spock came from Planet Parenthood
to replace the rod with Ritalin.
A marvelous land exiſts & I have been there
is the gist & thus far sober fact.
It does & he was.

[NOTE to Baron Munchausen:
hot-air balloon: "invented" by the Montgolfiers, a family of marbled-paper-
makers. Marbled paper was a hermetic discovery. Early balloons were
painted with hermetic emblems. Nadar the Photographer & pioneer
balloonist linked G. de Nerval, Baudelaire, Gautier, Nodier, Petrus Borel,
Parisian occultist circles. Ballooning as "Romantic Science" in the German
style of Novalis (& ultimately Paracelsus). Hot-air balloon a "neolithic
invention" as Paul Goodman called the bicycle (invented by L. da Vinci)
— i.e. used no techné unavailable to Stone Age. Classical writers (Lucian,
or certain Brahmanic Commentaries on the Rig Veda) suggest secret
of flight known to ancient magi. Modern technopathocracy replicates
fairy tale of Sorcerer's Apprentice, as Goethe foretold.]

ARTAUD TOMBEAU

Let no cop read this
rodomontade
        no one but
adepts who've completed
our mail-order course & received
        their decoder rings.
Besides, who cares?
Babbling decorticated dabbling
in electroshocking diablerie
-- O no
free speech belongs only to those
who are never heard or if heard
never believed or if believed then only
by fellow loons & ogres or
by the louse in yr coat,
              Artaud,
the parasite riding on yr reputation
for meaningless blather.

Time-Off For No Particular Behavior
A Tombeau for the Sultan

(Rafi Sharif, d. 2006)

The luxury of an empty day can only be compared to the pleasure
of an empty head — possibly our only hope for any Egypto-Moorish
immortality — sideways in Time — the death-defying slow leap
over Niagara, chained to a bear.
                    We're from the Fortean Society,
all we want is the damned facts, ma'am, just the mindless jubilation.
Or, failing that, at least a few empty titles, patents of extinct
nobility, admiralties in the Salvation Navy of a dying creed:
                                   Pop
Existentialist Entheogenic Ceremonialism for nietzschean nieces &
nephews, the Nth generation, masters of time travel but only in
one jerkwater minor alternate dimension.
                        And that was Baltimore in
the 50s — when secrets were secret — the heaven of trash — the
Isfahan of Alabama — horsewagons of ice & watermelons — a hopeless
Hafez — Thelonious Monk plays Mecca.
                          Emblem: in a marsh, a slack
shack on stilts on a pier on a bayou amid vast okeefenochian vistas
of tannic tarns & funereal mosses — the FitzOmarian "Thou", the
sly mockingbird, the slightly idiotic smile of the sky.

Shadow Unmanifesto

A few hours of crime compensate for a lifetime of civilized
stupefaction. Of always waiting for something else to happen.
You were the wolf, I know it, I saw you at the sabbat.

Only our secret phosphorescent backbones of sweet predations &
bad intentions can hold us up from slumping under the gravity of
this planet of stiffs.

Our ancestress was raped by a snake – now our clan can produce
supernatural poltergeistiche phenomena ad libitum.

This lascivious plainsong ripe as illegal cheese, this catalog of
venoms & tinctures in the collection of the Honorable So-&-So, this
record of burnt fingers & buried angels

speaks now in the hours of fusty hibernation, in the Hibernia or
Hyperborea of fecund boredom. Crimes remember us as we remember
you.

Gamblers' tells, mentalists' cues, Neapolitan shrugs, finger
alphabets, convicts' tappings, hobos' waymarks, runes,
Enochian petroglyphs

the "madness of two", languages from Mars, past life regressions,
alien sex cults: and you the Champollion the Dr Barry Fell of
gestural epigraphy alone will unearth my crimes, having understood
that this egg is my external soul.

CROM
Select Communiqués
of the
Cro-Magnon Liberation Front

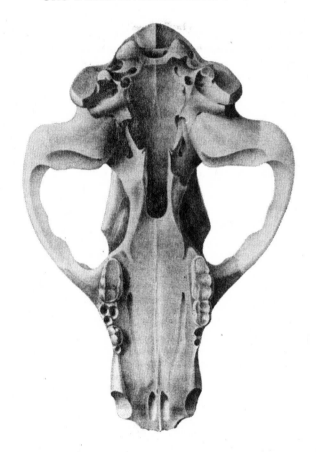

"This picture of a cave bear skull, seen from below, was published by Alexander von
Nordmann in 1858. Some of the teeth have fallen out, as shown by the empty root
sockets. Normally, there are three cheek teeth (one premolar and two molars)
on each side of the upper jaw, but in this specimen there is a small socket in front
of the left premolar, showing that it retained a vestigial extra premolar. The skull
belonged to a female individual, as shown by its relatively small dimensions and the
small sockets for the canine teeth (eyeteeth)."
— Björn Kurtén, *The Cave Bear Story: Life and Death of a Vanished Animal*
(NY: Columbia University Press, 1977).

Paleolithic engraving of a bear, probably *Ursus arctos*,
from the cave of Teyjat in Dordogne, France. After Koby. (Kurtén, *ibid*.)

I beseech my Hand-Stone
That it be not a flying shadow;
Be it a brand to rout the foes
In brave battle.
My fiery hard stone
Be it a red water snake
Woe to him around whom it coils
Betwixt the swelling waves.
Be it a sea eel
Be it a vulture among vultures
Which separate body from soul.
Be it an adder of nine coils
Around the body of gigantic Colpa
From the ground to his head,
The smooth spear-headed reptile.
The spear-armed royal stout wheel
Shall be as a galling strong thorny briar;
Woe is he around whom it shall come
My fiery stout powerful dragon.

(The Snake-Stone Spell of Mogh Roich, the
druid of Valencia Island & chief wizard of
Munster; in *Forbhais Droma Dámhgháire* from
The Book of Lismore, trans. Sean Ó Duinn)

CRO-MAGNON COMMUNIQUÉ #2

Lurid village gaslight stains
lowdown snow-gravid sky the color
of old port in crusted bottles but
transparent. The Cro-Magnon Peoples Army
prefers the cold coal tarry phosphorescence
of snow's own inherent luminosity
unbesmirched by metallurgy & its
contra-ESP emanations. Stone
for us is metaphormosis the very
stuff & bones of surgent biosis
weft to the warp of earth's flesh
& stone is night. We must blow up
the gas tower & revenge this injury
to the womb of revolution – our snow.

#9

Fiery Flying Roll

...let's go deeper...
...a bit more poison...

it's not just that space has texture – everyone knows how you
swim beneath gothic vaults or float in rainy deserted parks –
vortex spirals lifting dense squares into lark-like tenuity

& poison tells us that texture can itself be poisoned homeo-
pathically as with magical pepper: maleficently malignantly
buildings fall ill for no obvious reason – no mildew asbestos or
neon – simply from spatial necromancy.

Space is haunted by its own shape.

Over time local genies may
reshape whole landscapes & devas
reclaim polluted spaces changing
abandoned factories into instant
romantic ruins. Chaos favors beauty.
Entropy ennobles sweet disorder.

Somewhere in the Eighteenth Century it was decided that
since Hell doesn't exist it would be necessary to build it. Wel-
come to the bardo your book of the dead foretold O Osiris. We
are its nerves, its animated alphabet, your eternal wage slaves.

The akashic vibrations of plastic
are drastically Dracula-like.

You decry this nostalgism as if ready
                to defend your birthright of plastic & asphalt
against Vandals or Scythians in animal drag
                in chorus lines singing
                                take a hit of this baby &
                                bomb yrself back to the
        Stone Age
loom smashers
machine wreckers
hunt saboteurs &
poachers.

One day the costumed guides
                at the Stone Age Village Museum mutinied
                        threw the tourists overboard & sailed
permanently off into a shared séance of reversionism
        holding the Mastodon skeleton
                hostage. Back To the Caves
                        says the uprisen manifesto
                in unmovable type and
Voluntary Amorous Servitude
                that palpable tenderness of certain
                        atmospheres of beeswax
                                & sun dried laundry

ARMED NOSTALGIA

Defend that abandoned meadow
        that co-exists with yr very memory of it

PRE-AGRARIAN REVENGE

The hot air balloon is a perfectly Neolithic invention. Anyone
could have done it as soon as weaving was introduced. Elijah's
saucer was no extra-terrestrial UFO. Shamans literally flew on
giant kites from windswept mountain peaks. The crane shape
kites gave rise to legends of Taoist Immortals. Clay pots of fire
in night skies made silk globes luminesce like giant glowworms

Zeus from his chariot of cloud
hurled down greek fire upon
his enemies & called it
thunderbolts from heaven

THINK EUHEMERISTICALLY

Would you use a bomb to reactivate
your most explosive childhood
reveries?

Ibn Khaldun compares the sleep of nomads who wake at night
in the desert & look up at all the stars at once to that of animals
who sense the wind & darkness & fall back to sleep reassured
the universe is still there – but the city-dweller who travels by
caravan & sleeps al fresco in the wastelands wakes suddenly
into a gulf of stars & feels himself sucked into panic
freefall airless outer space.

Hermetic critique of light pollution reveals promethean
technopathology – Enlightenment as attempt to blot out the
stars with electromagnetic waves & carceral glare of all-nite
gas stations & bug zappers cutting off wage slave drones from
astral lustrations & dissipating aromal rays from planetary &
zodiacal deities to produce *textureless space* & permit necro-
mancers to vitiate & exhaust the vitality of night with vampiric
electricities & alien probes.

At last they barricaded themselves
into the Museum itself
& lay awake at night wondering if the
Anabaptists are right about technology could
they be right about theology too?
John the Baptist has that mauve &
tarnished silver look
that erotic gnosticism of the
desert cave as nocturnal egg.
Antinomian Anabaptist Neo-Luddite Rosicrucianism?
Would that have wings?

...a little little
more poison
and you can see how
swallows
over
the barn could
spiral
into
some non-euclidian
& yet quotidian
texture

CROM Communiqué #10

"Progress! What a
Belgian idea."
— Baudelaire

The Magus is enjoined to
make everything by hand – the wand
carved from tree the metals
mined & cast to the ad
absurdum. Sooner or later
you're using your mouth
as a third hand.
      Reversionism
casts a cloak of psychotronic
glamourie. A slinky toy.
A dégringolade toward Lascaux.
Kill lamb for parchment. Get
       out of jail free.
Capture the lightning in leyden jars.
As you move backward thru time
     you gain dark powers.

CROM Communiqué #20

CROM demands a Bureau of Endarkenment to whip up superstition. Peasants with scythes must riot against the Baron's tampering with electricity & corpses. Automobiles will be seen as monsters from hell even if it takes LSD in all the reservoirs. Penitenti yes let's have penitenti in black pointy hoods & robes scourging themselves across Bergmanesque landscapes of ruined factories. Thoreau was Cro-Magnon when he visualized ragweed & mushrooms pushing up thru asphalt & concrete "...forests...Indians..." his dying words. Ritual sledgehammers. Poetic Vandalism.

CROM Communiqué #28

You could do justice to this day
on a blackboard. The ice infects
the way to think like chalk on slate
like a chalk Hercules with
club & boner in Wiltshire or
whatever. Solve Problem With
Big Stick. Mentally we've got a
bonefire in the cavemouth & we're
lolling on pelts already. Snow
represents a lost mammoth shamanism
with clovis points & ritual huts
of mastodon ribs. Nothing human
outside the rockshelter. Only now
could we begin to speak in poetry.

ABOUT HAKIM BEY

"Who is Hakim Bey? I love him!" — Timothy Leary

"A Blake angel on bad acid" — Robert Anton Wilson

"Fascinating" — William S. Burroughs

"Lingusitic romp" — Colin Wilson

"Exquisite" — Allen Ginsberg

"...teaches a subtle and necessary science..." — Robert Kelly

"... raw bitter tender... for all humanity" — Anne Waldman

TAZ
THE TEMPORARY AUTONOMOUS ZONE,
ONTOLOGICAL ANARCHISM,
POETIC TERRORISM
Hakim Bey

The underground cult bestseller! Essays redefining the psycho-geographical nooks of autonomy. Recipes for poetic terror, anar-cho-black magic, post-situ psychotropic surgery, denunciations of spiritual addictions to vapid infotainment cults—this is the bas-tard classic, the watermark impressed upon our minds. Where conscience informs praxis, and action infects consciousness, *T.A.Z.* continues to worm its way into above-ground culture. Second edition, with a new introductory essay by the author and ad-ditional appendical materials.
ISBN: 1-57027-151-8 2003 160pp. 4½"x7" $9.95

Orgies of the Hemp Eaters
FIVE HUNDRED YEARS OF CANNABIS CUISINE, SLANG, RITUAL, LITERATURE

Hakim Bey and Abel Zug, editors

This "spiritual archeology" of pot history, science, folk-lore, cuisine, and *belles lettres* assembles the archive of the Western encounter with the "altered" indigenous Other, from North Africa to India and elsewhere. Includes one of the most comprehensive bibliographies of mari-juana literature ever assembled for the general reader.
ISBN: 1-57027-143-7 2004   694pp. 6"x9" $24.95

Millennium
Hakim Bey

In an interview and four additional essays, Hakim Bey explores how the blind panopticon of Capital remains most vulnerable in the realm of 'magic'—the manipulation of images to control events, hermetic "action at a distance."
ISBN: 1-57027-045-7 1996 128pp. 4½"x7" $9.95

Pirate Utopias
MOORISH CORSAIRS AND EUROPEAN RENEGADOES
Peter Lamborn Wilson

From the 16th to the 19th centuries, Moslem corsairs from the Barbary Coast ravaged European shipping and enslaved thousands of unlucky captives. During this same period, thousands more Europeans converted to Islam and joined the pirate holy war. Were these men (and women) the scum of the seas, apostates, traitors—Renegadoes? Or did they abandon and betray Christendom as a praxis of social resistance? Second edition, with new material documenting piracy in the very early days of New York City.

ISBN: 1-57027-158-5   2003   224pp.   4½"x7" $9.95

Avant Gardening
ECOLOGICAL STRUGGLES IN THE CITY AND THE WORLD
Peter Lamborn Wilson & Bill Weinberg, eds.

This collection of writings, assembled at a time of crisis for NYC community gardens, imagines the radical possibilities of urban gardening. Bringing together NYC history, political analysis, utopian schemes, poetic accounts of what gardening can create, and investigations into the dynamics of sustainability, community, high and low technologies, and power, this book challenges the "Supermarket to the World" ideologies of global capital. Includes work by Sarah Ferguson, Jack Collom, Carmelo Ruiz, the editors, and others.

ISBN: 1-57027-092-9   1999   176pp. 4½"x7" $9.95

Escape From the 19th Century
ESSAYS ON MARX, FOURIER, PROUDHON AND NIETZSCHE
Peter Lamborn Wilson

Did the nineteenth century ever come to an end? Was the twentieth century just a re-run? If to know "History" as tragedy is to escape its repetition as farce, then perhaps we need to look more deeply at this Past that won't stop haunting us. Two illuminated madmen—Charles Fourier and Friedrich Nietzsche—and two too-sane geniuses—J.-P. Proudhon and Karl Marx—are enlisted in the break-out plan. The shape of this plan is then suggested in a final essay showing how old "rights and customs" of paleolithic reciprocity and eqalitarian spirituality have made innumerable re-entries into History.

ISBN: 1-57027-073-2 1998 206pp. 6"x9" $14.95

Scandal
Essays in Islamic Heresy
Peter Lamborn Wilson

A search for the "poetic facts" of heresy in Islamic history, ranging from "sacred pederasty" in Persian sufism and forbidden imagery in Islamic art to the inner teachings of the Assassins, the heretical influences on Shiite terrorism, and the mystical uses of wine, opium, and hashish.
ISBN: 1-57027-156-9 1988 228pp. 6"x9 " $14.95

"Shower of Stars" — Dream & Book
The Initiatic Dream in Sufism and Taoism
Peter Lamborn Wilson

A tradition of intentional and initiatic dreaming, stretching from present-day dream-interpretation booklets back to ancient Sumerian and Egyptian practices, connects the Sufism of Ibn Arabi, medieval Kabalah, hemp-inspired Taoist scriptures, Afro-Brazilian spirit cults, and early Christian "angel alphabets." *Shower of Stars* pulls from this history specific methods of inducing prophetic or "true" dreams, with the purpose of achieving non-ordinary consciousness through autonomous openings to the world of the imagination.
ISBN: 1-57027-036-8 1992 192pp. 4½"x7" $9.95

Wild Children
Peter Lamborn Wilson & David Mandl, eds.

A "zine" exclusively by and for radical children ages 0–18. The only rule for *Wild Children* was that every young person who submitted material had at least one thing chosen for publication. We hoped to get some "uncensored" contributions, to hear young people speaking *for themselves*, not for parents, teachers, clergy, government agents, psychologists, or UNESCO "experts." And we were not disappointed!
ISBN: 0-936756-83-7 1992 64pp. 8½"x11" $5.95